Perry Roberts TRANSITION

Ikon Gallery, Birmingham
29 November 2006 – 21 January 2007

Exhibition curated by Nigel Prince

ISBN 1 904864 25 2

Ikon Gallery
1 Oozells Square, Brindleyplace, Birmingham, B1 2HS
t: +44 (0) 121 248 0708
f: +44 (0) 121 248 0709
http://www.ikon-gallery.co.uk
Registered charity no: 528892

Edited by Nigel Prince
Designed by Kim Beirnaert
Photography by Krystof Kriz, Jonathan Lee, Perry Roberts
Printed by Die Keure, Bruges (Belgium)

Distributed by Cornerhouse Publications
70 Oxford Street, Manchester, M1 5NH
publications@cornerhouse.org
t: +44 (0)161 200 1503
f: +44 (0)161 200 1504

All works courtesy of the artist

THE JOHN FEENEY
CHARITABLE
TRUST

Ministry of the
Flemish Community

Ikon gratefully acknowledges
financial assistance from Arts
Council England, West Midlands
and Birmingham City Council.

This exhibition is supported by
the Esmée Fairbairn Foundation,
the John Feeney Charitable
Trust, the Ministry of the Flemish
Community, Department of
Visual Arts and Museums.

IKON

TRANSITION

PERRY ROBERTS

Foreword

This is Perry Roberts' first solo exhibition in the UK since his departure from this country to take up residence in Belgium in the mid-1990s. It consists entirely of new work, commissioned by Ikon, made in response to architecture in Birmingham, characteristically encouraging us to look again at things we think we know.

Since his emergence as an artist, from Goldsmiths College, London in the late 1980s, Roberts has remained remarkably true to an aesthetic proposition that arises out of the problematic ideals of modernism. The smart minimalist tendency in his work betrays a fascination with an aesthetic paradigm that asserted universality and absolutes, and the assumption of cultural progress. On the other hand, this artist agonises over the necessity for choice... why this solution and not that one? How does anyone really know they are right? In the case of architecture, this is especially interesting, as choices in design can have such monumental consequences, subsequently affecting the lives of countless individuals who use and/or encounter the buildings that occur as a result. If the buildings are high-rise, as they tend to be in the heart of a city, the predicament is compounded.

On this occasion Roberts has made a number of video pieces focused on the exterior walls of large buildings, dating from the 1960s and 70s, identifiable in the agglomeration of Birmingham's city centre: a hotel, a library, a signal box, a car park and so on. The formal qualities, the configurations of lines and shapes on these skins stretched over supporting internal structures are eloquent, very telling through their modernist references. The grids, the pre-fab repetitions, the "abstract" vernaculars – these all suggest a kind of certainty supposed to come with science and mathematics. Furthermore, they share a visual vocabulary that is the inspiration for the style Roberts adopts, the style that he takes and reinserts into a loose-knit, global conversation about art and the way it fits into everyday life. In the videos we see the difference made to the appearance of architecture by the sun moving through the sky. Shot on clear days, we see (through time-lapse) highlights and shadows shift around the regular criss-crossing textures that make up this local urban fabric. These are sheer, fugitive images of static and substantial subjects. The camera and the buildings don't move, but clearly here we have a question of lighting courtesy of a source beyond our built environment. Roberts is reminding us of the fact that time passes – that, in fact, everything on Earth is a sun-dial – that lives are lived through and around these places, and our apprehension of the familiar is determined (absolutely) by particular circumstances.

It is vital, incidentally, to have architectural circumstances here in Birmingham – manifested in the various buildings of artistic organisations, such as Ikon – that enhance such philosophical reflection. For this we are grateful to Arts Council England and Birmingham City Council, and with regard to this exhibition, as part of our overall mission, we are indebted to The Esmée Fairbarn Foundation, The John Feeney Charitable Trust and the Ministry of the Flemish Community (Belgium), Department of Visual Arts and Museums. Above all, we count our blessings for the intelligence and sensibility of artists such as Perry Roberts.

Jonathan Watkins
Director

Observations on architecture and the 1960s

The 1960s was an exciting decade when Britain finally broke out of the dismal utilitarian aftermath and economic gloom of the immediate post-war years. Social, economic and political change created opportunities for new and innovative solutions to meet a massive programme of regeneration and construction of the urban fabric of our towns and cities.

The world was changing rapidly and architects working in the 60s were challenged to create new building and urban design solutions in response to these demands.

Schools and houses were required not only to replace destroyed or sub-standard pre-war buildings, but also to accommodate the post-war population explosion and the enhanced expectations of an increasingly affluent society.

Better housing, factories and offices and shopping facilities with an improved urban infrastructure; these pressures created new opportunities, new challenges in almost every aspect of human activity.

As a result, far from its much maligned image today, the 60s was a decade that encouraged innovative design not just in architecture but also in other areas – Carnaby Street fashion, the Mini skirt and the Mini car, Concorde and the explosion of universal air travel. What an exciting creative decade!

Bigger and better office buildings appeared, not just in central London but also in the cheaper suburbs and the centres of regional cities such as Birmingham, Manchester and Leeds.

Redeveloped or extended town centres incorporated ever larger retail stores, larger and larger supermarkets as well as traditional small local traders. High Streets increasingly became car-free pedestrianised zones.

Building designed to accommodate off-street car parking cleared increasingly congested urban roads for the users of these buildings and improved access for the growing numbers and size of delivery lorries servicing larger and more complex developments.

Dealing with this explosion of traffic required improved roads, by-passes, ring roads and motorways. The M1 provided efficient and reliable road access to and from London and Birmingham. Motorway extensions soon covered most of the UK leading to the need for complicated motorway intersections such as Spaghetti Junction.

The construction industry was changing. Increased prefabrication starting with the immediate post war "temporary" housing expanded into all aspects of building. Windows, doors, external wall cladding, internal partitions previously constructed on-site were produced to standardised design manufactured to higher quality in off-site factories.

Traditional construction methods and materials adapted to meet these new requirements. New materials created opportunities for imaginative design solutions to meet the developing needs of the 60s.

Concrete, the main structural material for multi-storey buildings, was more widely used as a facing material with varying surface finishes; smooth fair faced with little texture, a timber grain finish formed by the temporary shutter boards that held the wet concrete in place. Heavily indented vertical grooves in pre-cast concrete panels provided an interesting and continually changing surface texture.

The so-called concrete "brutalist" architecture of the 1960s was greatly influenced by a three-dimensional "cubist" design approach to function – a multi-level

integrated use of rectangular volume with a clear expression of the concrete structure that supported that space. Exposed structural concrete as the dominant external material was used as a powerful cohesive frame into which many and various minor features and activities would fit.

The result was strong structures creating visually powerful urban statements. Bold interlocking three-dimensional multi-level spaces with projections and recessions externally creating a pattern of light and shade with continually changing vistas and views. The inclusion of a strong selective use of colour to define and articulate the building – both externally and internally – created a new design dimension.

Markedly different aesthetically was the almost universal and not always very imaginative use of the glass curtain wall. A surface texture created mainly by the light and shade on metal glazing bars dividing the smooth, hard and reflective glass. At night a speckled pattern of lit and unlit rooms and floors silhouetted against the dark night sky.

Much of what was built during that decade, particularly commercial and industrial buildings was built too quickly and too cheaply. In the public sector this certainly applied to much of the council housing built in this period. The pressures for more and more, faster and faster, cheaper and cheaper led to the use of often crudely designed and badly built high-rise concrete slab council housing and to disasters such as Ronan Point.

Today 60s buildings are almost universally and often unjustifiably denigrated. They are judged against the needs of today rather than whether they met the demands at the time they were conceived and built. Forty years on most buildings are obsolete and should be replaced or require major refurbishment to bring them up to the requirements of the 21st century.

Yet there is now a growing appreciation that not all 60s buildings are as bad as the media at times portrays. A far more objective judgement has emerged based on an understanding of the potential for retention and modernising rather than the "lynch mob" mentality of those who call for their immediate demolition, too often without ensuring in advance replacement development will be better than renovating what exists.

But these 60s buildings are there until they are rejuvenated or demolished as part of the normal pattern of urban regeneration. They are for good or bad part of the existing urban environment. Many are visually unmissable.

A better public understanding of how these buildings, which are part of our everyday lives, can be improved will help guide those who are responsible for the decisions to adapt and improve, or demolish and replace.

Owen Luder
CBE PPRIBA

Note

Owen Luder CBE, Past President Royal Institute of British Architects, established himself as an innovative architect in the 60s with a number of award winning buildings that over time have become both heavily criticised and controversial. Best known are the multi-level Tricorn Shopping Centre in Portsmouth (now demolished) and the multi-storey car park and shopping centre in Gateshead immortalised in the film *Get Carter* starring Michael Caine.

Under the sun

In the 1960s and 1970s many UK cities underwent rapid development on an unprecedented scale in terms of building and road construction. One such example is Roberts' hometown, where the legacy of T. Dan Smith, 'Mr. Newcastle', lives on. With a vision close to the urban regeneration programmes of today, his pioneering dream of a 'Brasilia of the North', rivalling other great cities of the world, was breathtaking. During the same period Birmingham was described in 1970 as a city where action had replaced words and the foundations were being laid for one of the most visually dynamic and exciting cities in Britain. However, opinions were soon to change and throughout the UK, as this version of urbanism was discredited, so cities and buildings of the era became identified with its worst excesses and failures – perfect examples of the dystopian image of urban decline. The once booming environments, all-encompassing of such ambitious and progressive vision, initially generators of considerable commercial activity, soon converted into reputations as ugly, car-friendly, post-industrial nightmares. Surrounded by the so-called 'concrete collars' of inner ring roads and motorways, epitomised in Birmingham by the intersection known as 'Spaghetti Junction', architects and planners were seen to have failed, buildings and civic space divorced from the function demanded by its citizens; the freedom proposed by modernity, implicit in such structures, sadly unrealised.

Decades later, as shopping and leisure arenas supplanted regions of manufacturing industry, many of these cities embraced the need for change and are now in the process of transforming, poised somewhere between decline and regeneration, offering a contrasting and fascinating combination of the old, the not so old and the new. Scattered across Britain, architectural reminders of this major post-war redevelopment stand out, not always sitting comfortably in their modified surroundings. Often they have a spare beauty. In Birmingham, a leading example is the Central Library in Chamberlain Square, the major surviving building by the John Madin Design Group. An inverted concrete ziggurat, described by some as the ugliest building in the city, its current status is uncertain and original condition diluted by unsympathetic commercial new-build in its public piazza, the ironically named 'Paradise Circus'.

Elsewhere in Birmingham is the Jury's Inn Hotel, formerly Chamberlain Tower, a huge concrete monolith that dominates the skyline in the neighbourhood of Ikon; the glass and marble office block, former headquarters of the Post and Mail, for so long empty and decaying, has now been demolished despite being the earliest UK example of podium and slab design, yet the equally significant signal box at New Street station has been listed. In Sheffield, a future for Park Hill is secured through energetic refurbishment schemes, but in Portsmouth the Tricorn Centre is no longer. In general these buildings are often despised as reminders of a time when cities were under siege by modernism and 'the good old days' were being concreted over. By focusing on these structures, Roberts calls into question our relationship to the built environment shaping our daily lives and reflects upon the part it plays in our shifting experiences of the everyday.

Roberts cites his formative years in the north east of England as the origin for his preoccupation with issues surrounding architectural reference. His daily routine in Gateshead took him past both the Trinity Centre Multi-Storey car park and Derwent Tower, known locally as 'The Dunston Rocket' due to its distinctive form, both designed by Owen Luder, one of Britain's foremost post-war architects and also designer of the Tricorn Centre. The car park opened in 1969 and, famous for its inclusion in the gritty 1971 film *Get Carter*, is a prime example of the brutalist aesthetic in raw concrete. It too now faces threat of demolition. Roberts describes initial thoughts on these iconic buildings as fantastical; at the beginning of the 1970s it was akin to encountering some futuristic alien presence in their challenge to the existing topography of the north east. This is the impetus – architecture that seemed simultaneously a part of but apart from the city – that has consistently drawn him to such structures. That they were often built in isolation, and at times replaced buildings that should have been kept, aids their uncompromising stance, paradoxically consigning them to a negative reception remote from the rest of the city. If afforded a more immediately sympathetic context and environment, perhaps a positive response would be forthcoming.

Early works by Roberts were prompted in particular by the post-modern tendency to clad buildings, the external feature of brick or stone being 'hung' from steel armatures as a façade. His 'paintings', often multi-layered, reference a type of prefabricated, modular form asserting a connection to architecture and whose panelling speaks of sequential progression. They suggest the potential for endless extension and contain a sense of their own

Untitled 1991
120 x 120 x 15 cm
cotton canvas, linen and black canvas

Untitled wall drawing 1991
21 x 4,5 m
Chisenhale Gallery, London

history; evidence of the passing of time is inherent in their making. In his series of monumental wall drawings, the first installed at Chisenhale Gallery, London in 1991, direct relationships to architecture are made with configurations derived from the locations, histories and buildings containing them. Often the painted surfaces and grids imply an underlying construction which in turn recalls the timber frame beneath three-dimensional work employing variously coloured untreated canvas. New works have moved away from the 'fixed' objects, more literally developing a fresh dimension to his practice while retaining its essential propositions, taking as their source the type of concrete buildings from the late 1960s he encountered as a teenager.

In 1997-98 Roberts produced a series of works titled *Twenty-four hour paintings*. These were his first pieces specifically dealing with light as a physical phenomenon. Stretched linen canvases, the raw material visible save for four small rectangles of differing 'browns' butted against the edges, were made. These colours relate to the perceived shade of the linen on different occasions such as early morning or late evening, each 'disappearing' into the fabric support when viewed at the appropriate time of the day. Later works also reveal the attributes of light through the use of different whites, juxtapositions tinted with a palette of earth colours reliant on light to enable their similarity and difference to be seen. With these sequences Roberts again returns us to the

24 hour painting 2000
200 x 100 cm
acrylic and gesso on linen

Untitled 2001
200 x 200 cm
acrylic on polyester

locus of concerns in his work – an opening up to the possibilities of more than one solution, the perception of a unique standpoint is questioned, and the balance between opposition and equilibrium. Reflecting on his practice leads us to the consideration that there are no absolutes, the particular is but one option, opinion is more about position and attitude. His *Untitled* series, including black paintings, present a lozenge moving outside of the pictorial space, introducing meditation on something outside of the frame. It reiterates the notion that what is seen is not always a singular thing, and by underlining the idea of the snapshot, recalls a link to photography.

In his most recent works, sequences of stills produce animations encompassing gradual movement shot over extensive periods of time, their focus being the exteriors of a number of buildings in Birmingham. Each frame making up individual pieces captures fractions of seconds invisible to the naked eye, unseen changes at the heart of the city. On-going preoccupations engaging with issues of modernity, centred on a contemplation of the urban fabric – notions of progress, figuration versus abstraction, reduction in form and interiority versus exteriority – are retained and amplified. These new films expand the potential of his wall drawings and three-dimensional pieces, and heighten the fixation on façade to something more robust. It is important to recognise the aesthetic value of the graphic composition and its discrete objecthood as distinct from the function of the depicted buildings. The city is pictured reduced to abstract pattern. The visual sensation of form, shape, tone, surface and being shown as projection are of equal value, of this and that.

By careful consideration of the relationship between particular source imagery and the scale and positioning of its presentation, so Roberts establishes a kinetic relationship between the viewer, his work and the city at large, allowing for a physical as well as conceptual response based on shifting perceptions. We must call upon our memory of the metropolis and our own experience within its structures in order to engage with the complexity of the work, and as such this extends the condition of his earlier three-dimensional pieces. Here, the audience could only comprehend the whole of the 'painting' by moving around it, this movement revealing the construction and differently coloured fabric layers, figure and ground becoming equal and exchangeable.

During research visits for this exhibition throughout 2005, a preliminary selection of suitable buildings and locations was made. Roberts has a personal connection to Birmingham and his return prompted recognition of the familiar oddly disturbed due to vast expanses of regeneration. Having absorbed the qualities of space and various landmarks throughout the mid 1980s, he re-established a dialogue with this half-remembered city and, carrying visual memories of the North East, was inclined to focus on buildings reminiscent from formative years. Their construction, form and material provided echoes to characteristics of earlier work; Roberts was struck by the still-contemporary pattern and surface of these forms of modernism and now, with appropriate distance, was interested in looking again, confronting these overlooked structures so long the brunt of popular criticism, the bête noire of a particular brand of urbanism.

The process of Roberts' orientation with the city, absorbing its information, allowing time to unfold before deciding how to make sense of the opportunity, is a factor akin to the experience of viewing the work; we not only confront it in the present but understand it through time. The object, its subject and its means of presentation are conflated into occupying the same space; the city is at once the artwork, the work, the real world of the city, both reliant for interpretation on our ever-changing experiences. As Roberts has stated previously, his works "are not pure forms representing utopian values… Instead they rely for their meaning on knowledge of the world, and the objects within it."

Through editing, framing and manipulation of images, the filmed architecture is simultaneously recognisable yet generalised; the concrete becomes animate, rippling with light and shade, sometimes contradicting the structure, sometimes enhancing its form. Its sense of solidity and weight remain and yet are oddly fluid. We become aware of light itself as a distinct substance playing across the surface of the structures. And time passes while little seems to alter; concrete forms remaining intact, untouched by the fleeting hours. Their monolithic form, the monumentality of their construction reinforces readings of permanence, yet the scale and pace of change revealed by the transient elements of weather and light sits in contrast to their often threatened state through fashion and regeneration.

The passage of the sun, its slow, constant, enduring rhythm, sits in counterpoint to the frenetic interweaving of the city and its populace. Light caresses its buildings, defining in gentle, generous gestures. The new films by Roberts expose the nature of this transition and, by being looped, physically and conceptually mirror the on-going circularity. Minutes pass, hours go by, the earth spins on its axis and revolves about the sun, and in the midst of this we go about our daily lives. By working with sequences of images rather than making more conventional films, Roberts proposes these as akin to a succession of moments; a series of truths that are constantly changing, shifting vistas, and as such can be seen as parallel territories to the serial imagery from Monet's *Haystacks, Gare Saint-Lazare* or *Rouen Cathedral*. Here motifs remain constant, enabling a concentration on that which is ephemeral.

Due to the nature of their largely prefabricated construction, the individual buildings chosen have a particular structural rhythm, visually linked to each other through their distinctive 'texture'. Roberts used digital time-lapse photography to record the passage of sunlight over their surfaces revealing how light helps to define this quality, giving each building its sculptural form and unique character. The intention is not to romanticise but to reveal a phenomenon not obvious in real time. Roberts is concerned to avoid any sentimentality and further is not campaigning to champion one building style over another. Instead he asks us to reconsider our position, suggesting everything might be worthwhile. By not identifying the specific buildings, showing only abstracted details concentrating on the graphic qualities of their exterior surfaces, and being projected actual size, invitations are intimated whereby, as a viewer, we can re-evaluate each subject and through this, re-engage with the environment and contemplate the valuable contribution such buildings make to the overall visual complexity of a city.

These films also inject a new sense of narrative into the environment and, in contrast to his earlier wall drawings and three-dimensional objects, evoke a different kind of emotive response to the places and spaces in which we play out our lives. The spare and economic use of edited visual information counters any inferred drama that would emerge, the commonplace hustle and bustle resolutely remaining outside of the frame, an inappropriate referent; in its place a breadth of poignant concerns surfaces, reverberating with our experiences over the passage of time.

The selection of an architectural fragment by Roberts, a further articulation of his insistence upon the lack of an authoritarian singular, may be the only way to express or provide clues to the future. Lost in the constant building and re-building, a city seeks to present definitive models of living space and yet consistently, inevitably, creates many seemingly ideal versions. By failing to make one all-pervasive image or dominant representation, remnants of each successive attempt remain. This mishmash paradoxically signifies a city's success, manifesting diversity and a richer, more complex dialogue between constituent cultures through time. It is this that is carried forward to become an unending contemporary experience.

Nigel Prince
Curator

JURY'S INN

HOTEL

Ian Fraser, John Roberts & Partners 1974 – 75
formerly Chamberlain Tower

DAVEN
BREWERY

PORTS

EXTENSION

Demolished 2006

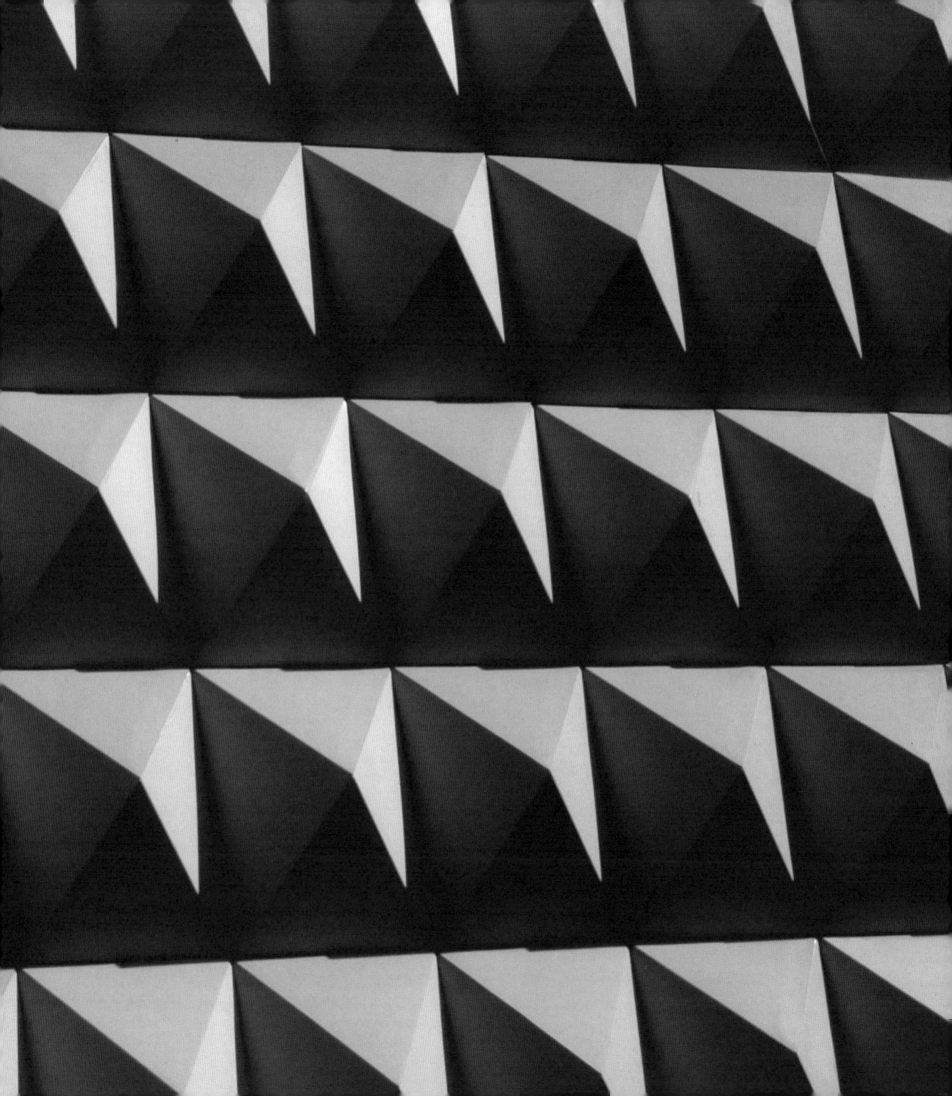

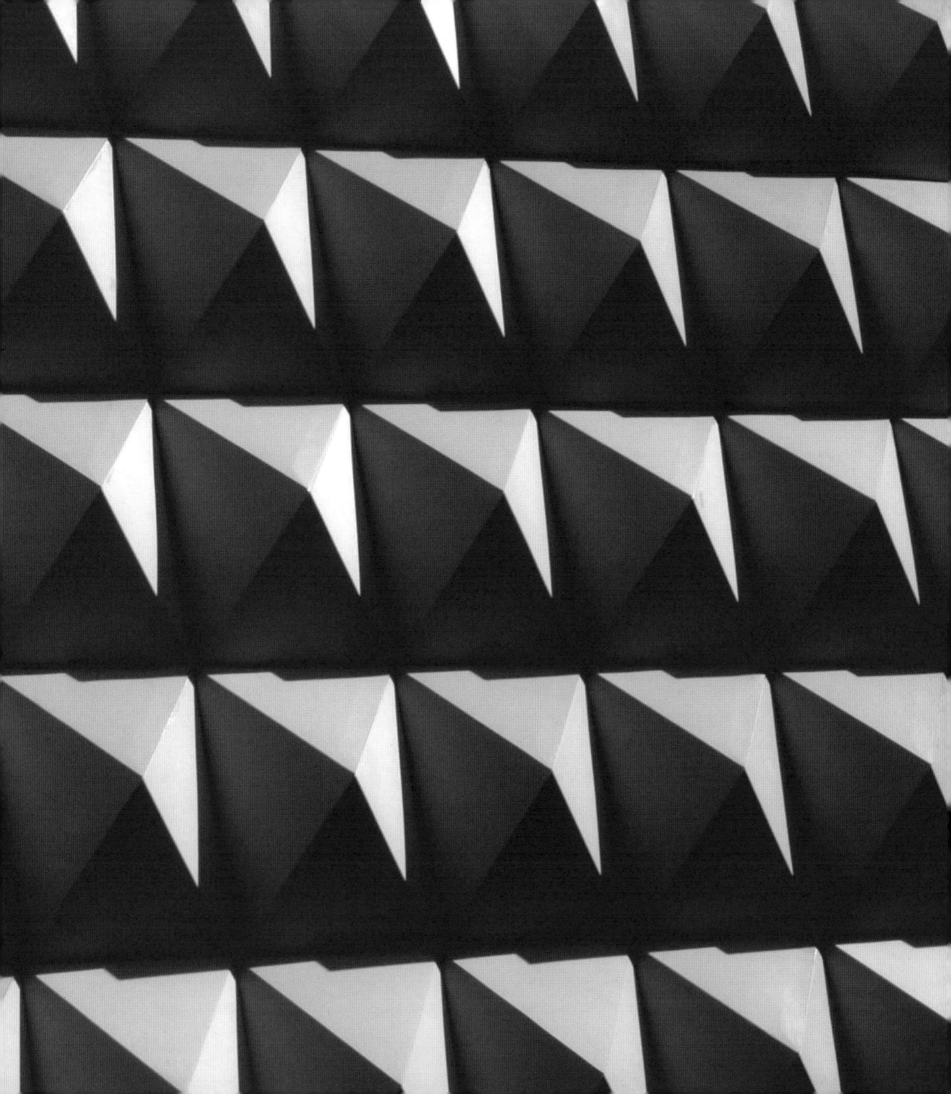

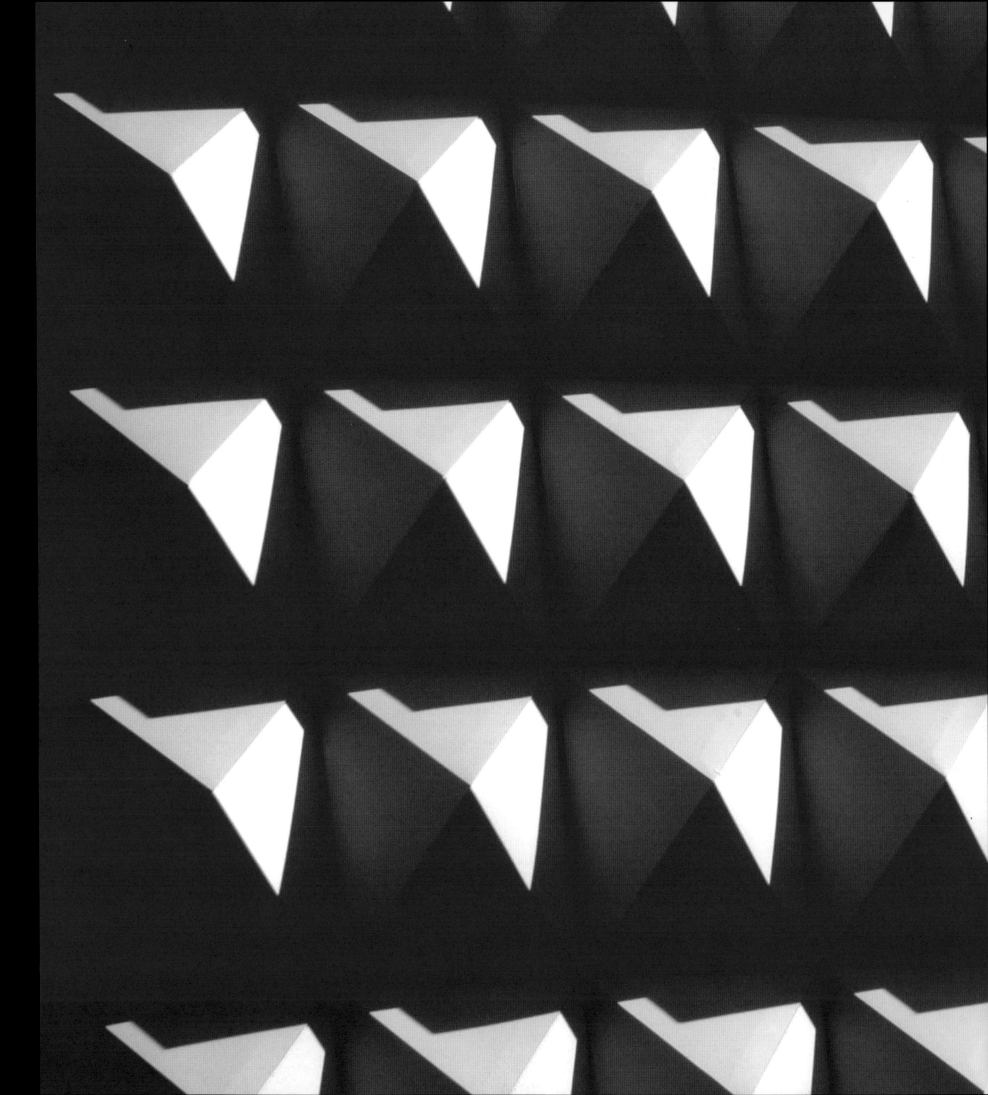

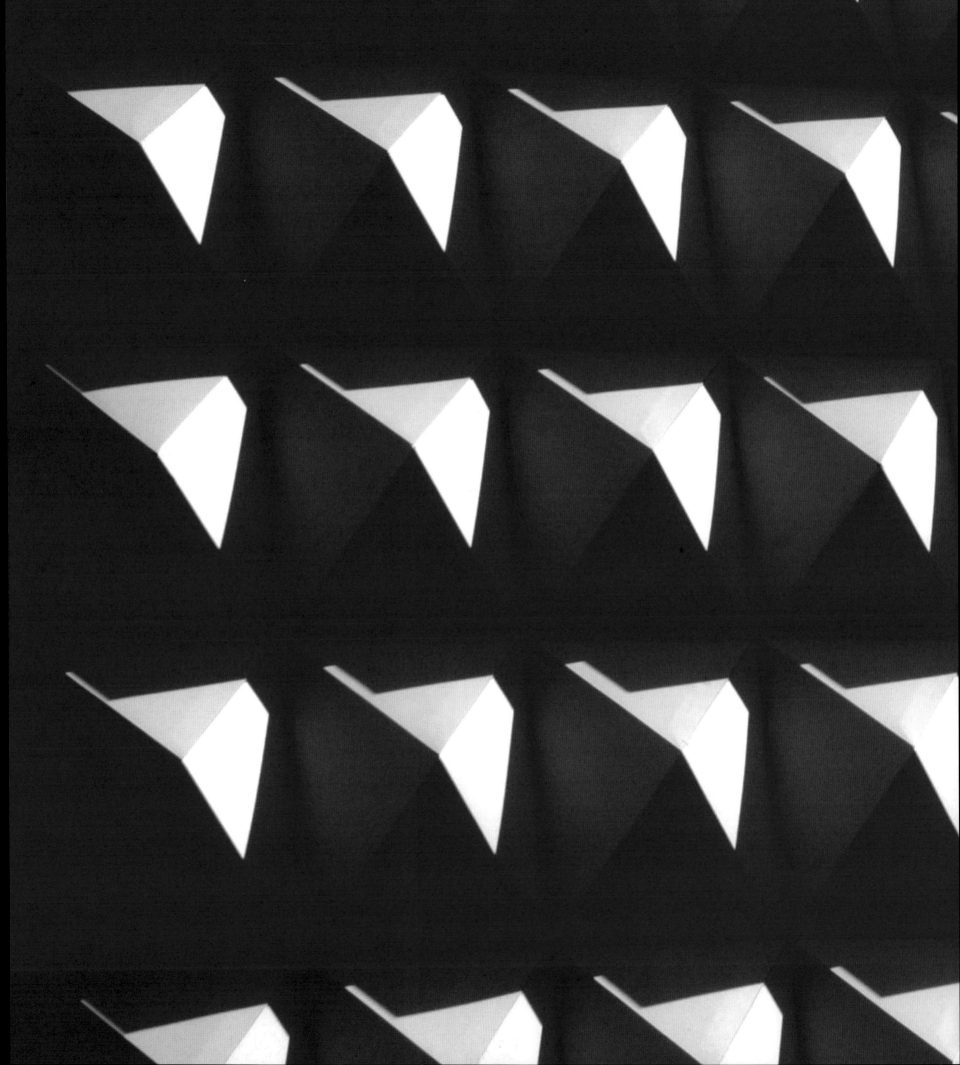

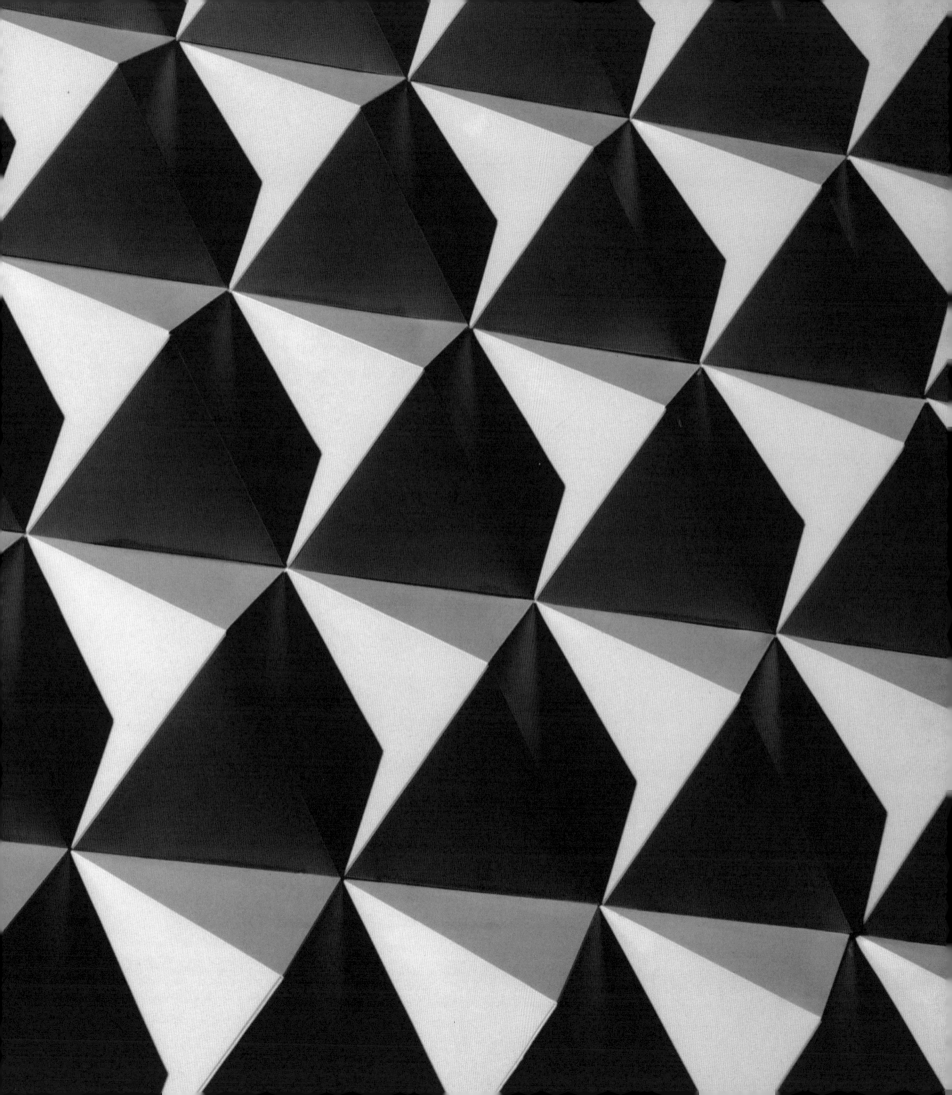

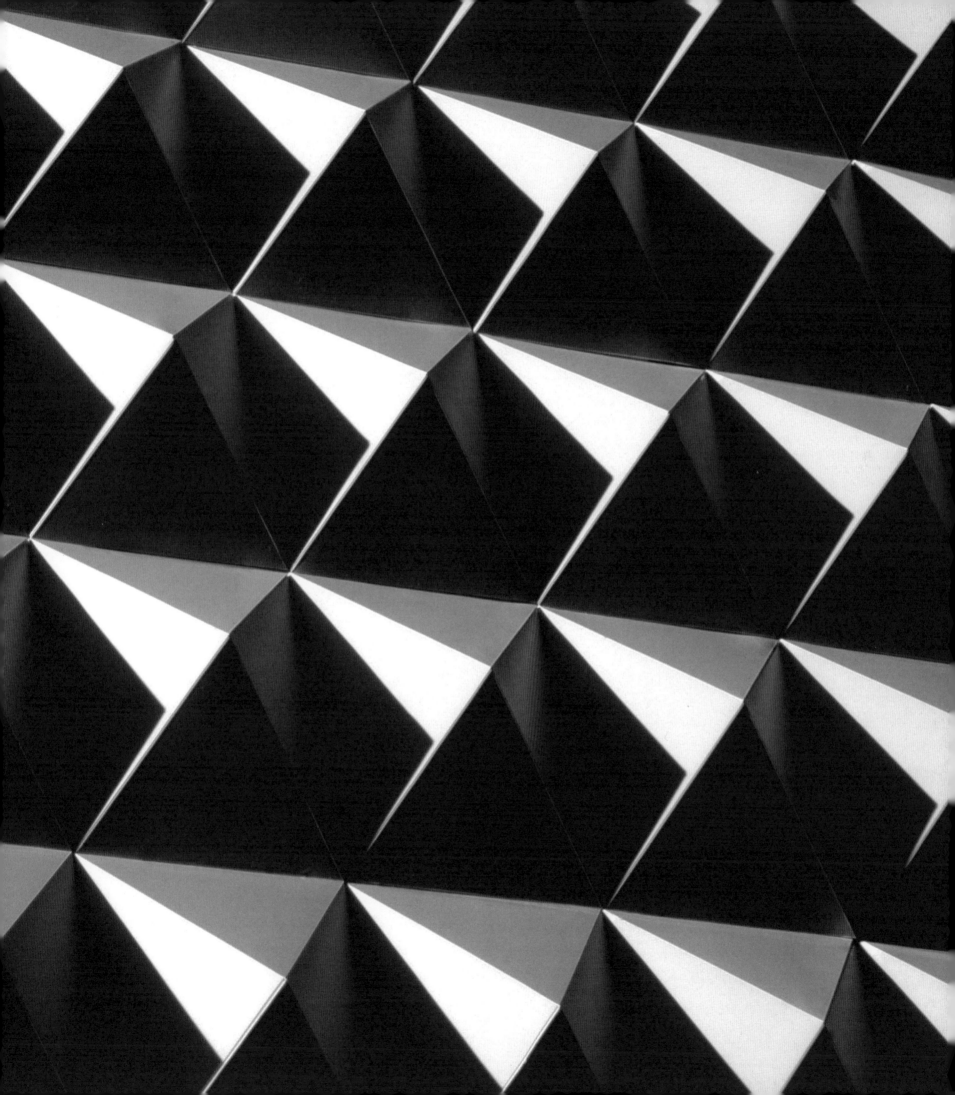

SIGNAL BOX

**Bicknell & Hamilton with
W.R. Headley,
Regional Architect,
British Railways London
Midland Region
1964 – 65**

NEW STREET STATION

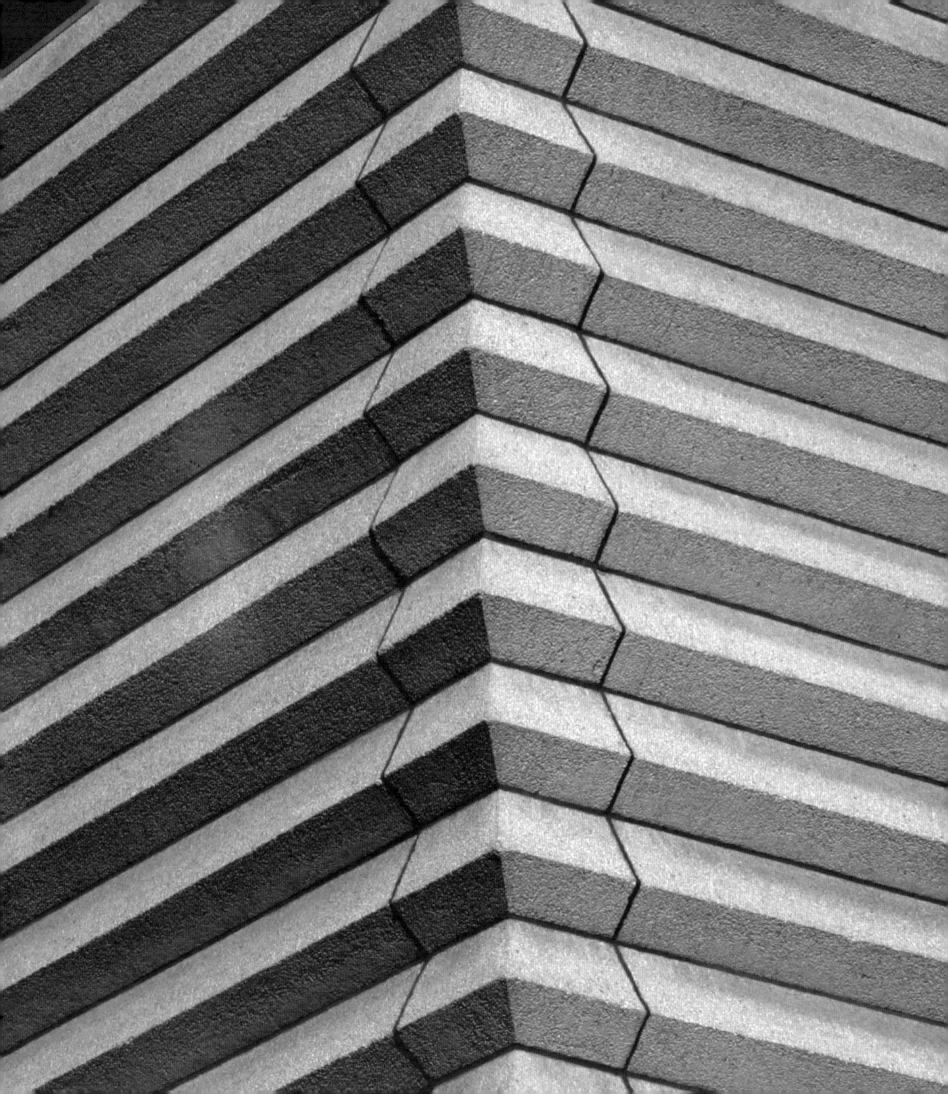

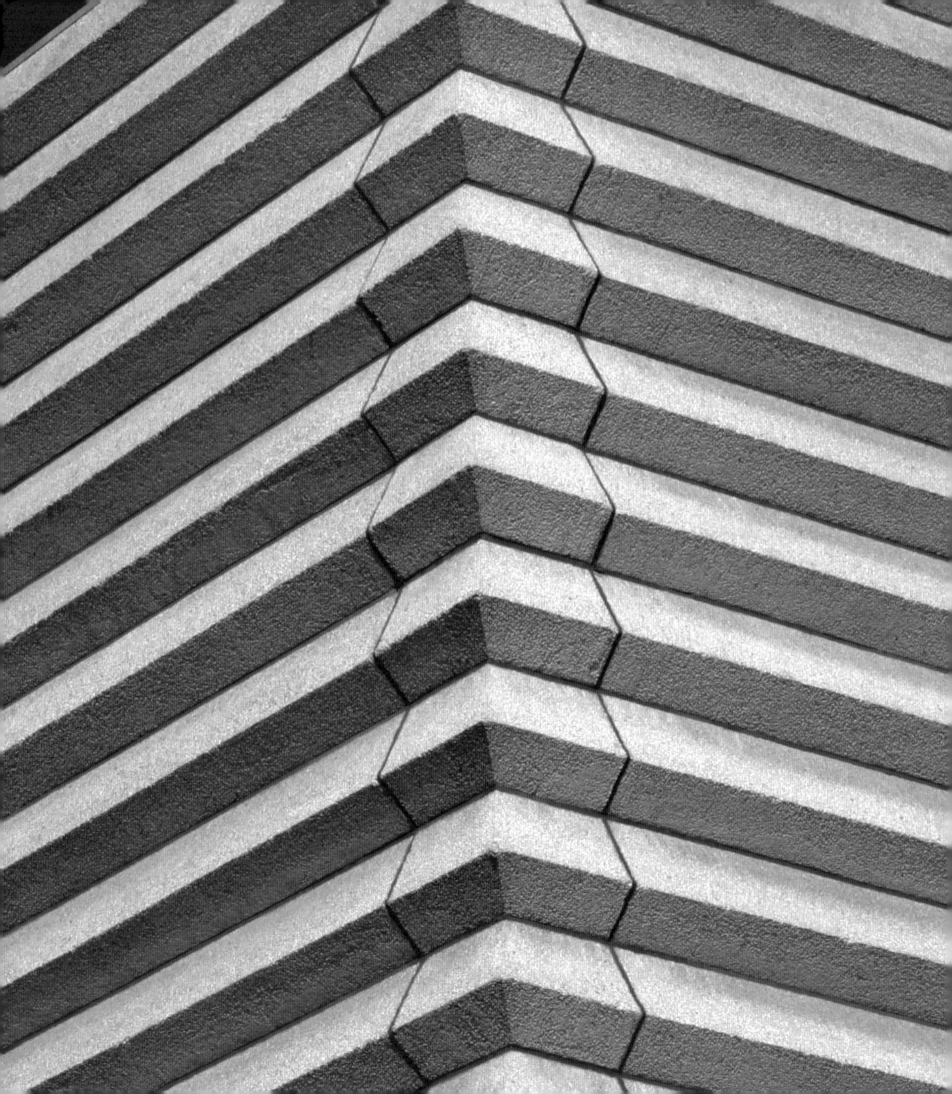

BIRMI

John Madin Design Group
Designed 1964 – 66; built 1969 – 74

NGHAM

CENTRAL

LIBRARY